YOU CAN
COUNT ON ME

HASITHA AND SANDUNIKA

Story by Sandunika Dissanayake and Hasitha Nuwan
Illustrated by Sandunika Dissanayake
Formatted by Hasitha Nuwan
Edited and mentored by Nadishka Aloysius

Paperback: ISBN: 978-624-94918-1-6
Hardcover: ISBN: 978-624-94918-2-3
Ebook : ISBN: 978-624-94918-0-9

Visit www.flyawaytales.com for more information.

This book
belongs to
ECKY
STELLA

To our dear friends,
the ones we can always count on for a
laugh, a hand, and even the most delightfully
absurd solutions.
You're the best!

YOU CAN
COUNT ON ME

Once upon a time, in a cozy little drawer lived colorful and beautiful socks.

They were best of friends.

But poor Solo didn't have a best friend. She was
sad and lonely.

She never got to go out because she didn't have
a best friend to go with.

Why would anyone go with
a single sock?

Solo watched her sock friends go to the laundry and come back all clean and shiny.

But she was left behind, feeling sad and wondering,

Why don't they pick me too?

Every night, the other socks would gather and excitedly talk about their daily adventures.
Today we played soccer !
We played last week too!

But Solo? She had no stories to share.
She felt left out and very sad.

One day, the other socks gathered
around Solo and teased her.

You don't know how beautiful the outside world is!
You are so boring!
Solo felt really hurt!

But Dotty and Spotty felt bad. They didn't like seeing Solo sad.

They wanted to help but didn't know how.

They thought a lot, trying to come up with a plan.

Let's tie them up so they can't say mean things Anymore!

How about throwing them into a **puddle** when we are on the clothesline?

Hmm...
but we are just being the same as them.

Let's make a
sock slide to carry
her out!

But will the
other socks
help?

I'm not
sure!

How about
a paper plane?
But what if she
gets lost?

I have a better idea. Let's paint dots on her to look like us, then we can take turns going out!
WOW! That's a brilliant idea!
They cheered excitedly.

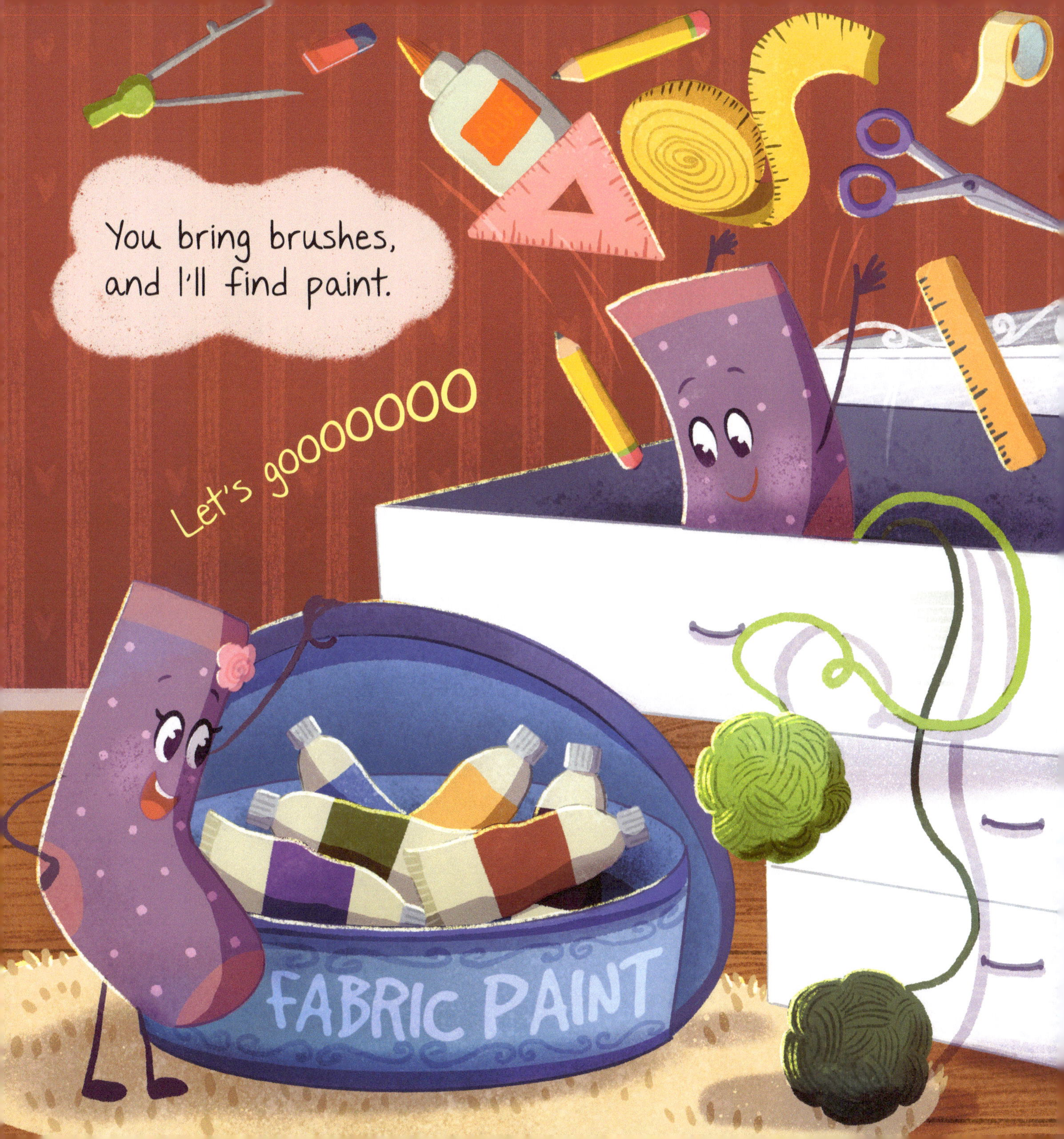

You bring brushes, and I'll find paint.
Let's gooooooo
FABRIC PAINT

They dipped their brushes in paint, and carefully painted Solo with dots, just like their own.

At the end, Solo looked just like Dotty and Spotty.

The next morning, guess what?

Solo was picked to go out with Dotty, just like they planned!

They were super excited.

She was overjoyed to see the world
beyond the drawer. Everything
looked so magical!

Solo enjoyed getting splashed in the puddles. It was so much fun!

She was amazed to touch the soft grass and smell the sweet flowers.

Solo met lots of new friends!
Some were tall, some were short.
Oh wait! Some even had head bands.

And **Surprise!**

She was even taken to the laundry. She had never looked better, so clean and shiny!

Now Solo also has stories to share with others. She shared her adventures passionately.

The other socks felt ashamed for teasing her.

We were mean! But Dotty and Spotty sacrificed their turns so that Solo could have fun! That's what **true friendship** is all about! We shouldn't let our friends down when they need help!

They understood.

From that day on, they all remembered to be kind and help each other whenever they could.

And Solo? Well, she was never lonely again.

She had buddies whom she could count on anytime, and they all lived happily ever after.

THE END

Check out other books of The Socks series.

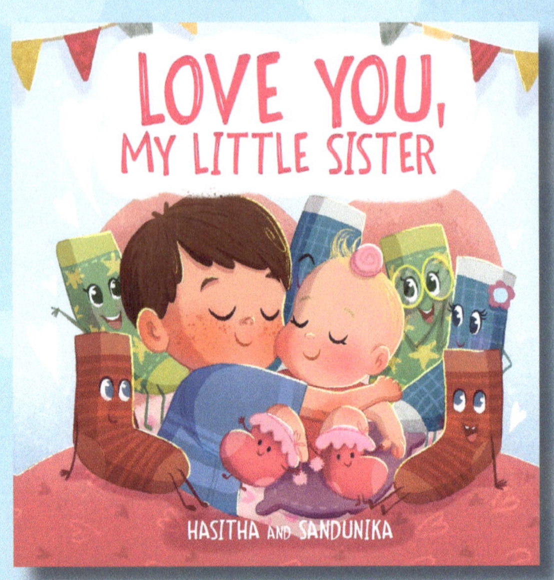

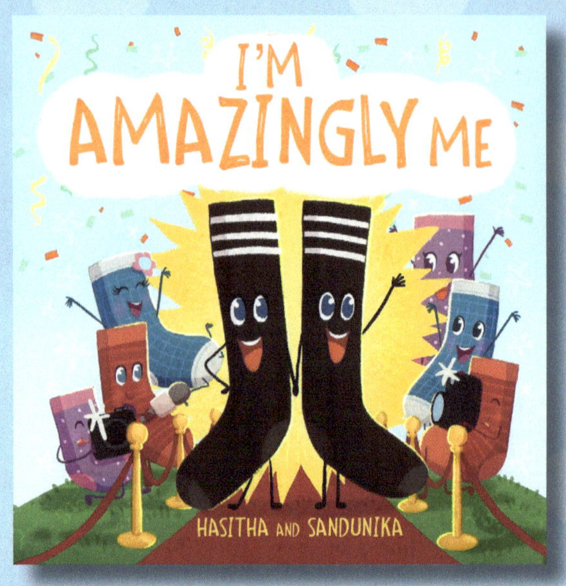

Thank you for reading the book!
If you enjoyed the book, we would greatly appreciate it
if you could take a moment to write an honest review on
Amazon. Your kind feedback means a lot to us.
Thank you!

For the **FREE AUDIOBOOK**, latest deals and new releases,
be sure to subscribe to our newsletter.
Sign up at www.flyawaytales.com